Paras

Bless you both with lots of fun filled
experience which will help you to
our liver.

love,

Sita Muljala

10/24/09

INDIA

I humbly dedicate this book, with love and respect, to my grandfather, Chundru Veerannagaru, who used to sing Vemana poems, and to my grandmother Chundru Seshayammagaru, who in turn encouraged me to try and expand my talents. Also to my father Chundru Rajugaru, who used to affectionately compliment me as Saraswathi!

What is Vemana Saying?

Read for yourself!

Children's Stories Illustrating Universal Values

Sita Mutyala

Sita Mutyala
Illustrated by Sireesha Amaram

Vol. I

WeShine Press Co

Text © 2009
Sita Mutyala

Illustrations © 2009
Sireesha Amaram

Published by WeShine Press Co
12 Lake Mist Drive
Sugar Land, Texas 77479
WeShinePress@yahoo.com
www.WeShinePress.com

Editors
Sireesha Mutyala
Swapna Reddy

Printed and bound by Kalajyothi in India
First Edition – 2009

ISBN: 978-0-9818113-0-7
Library of Congress Control Number: 2008928929

Publisher's Cataloging-in-Publication Data
Mutyala, Sita Chundru, 1949 -

What is Vemana Saying?
By Sita Mutyala
Illustrated by Sireesha Amaram

32 p. 26 cm.
Includes poems in Telugu script,
pronunciations and definitions

Summary: Stories demonstrate universal
values for children to remember

1. Vemana
2. Kindness
3. Equality
4. Sharing

177.2 -----dc22

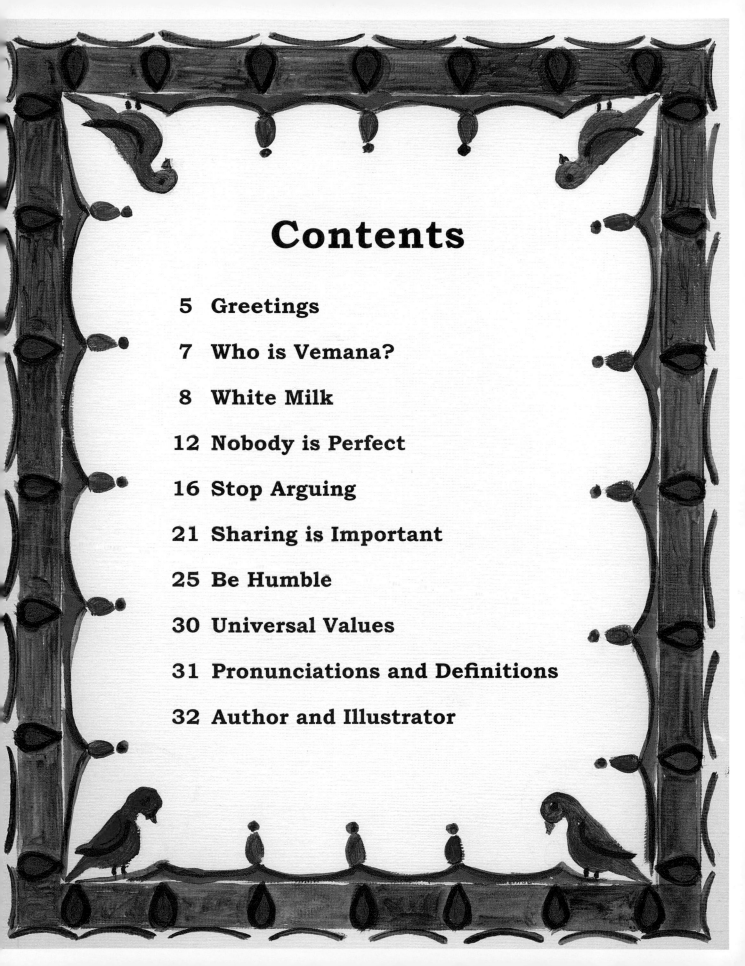

Contents

Greetings

Are you ready to find out who Vemana is and what he is saying?

Look for a special message in each interesting story.

Remember these important values every day and throughout your life.

That is what growing is all about!

Each Vemana poem is shown in the Telugu script, how to pronounce it, and its English translation. Following is a story demonstrating the message of each poem.

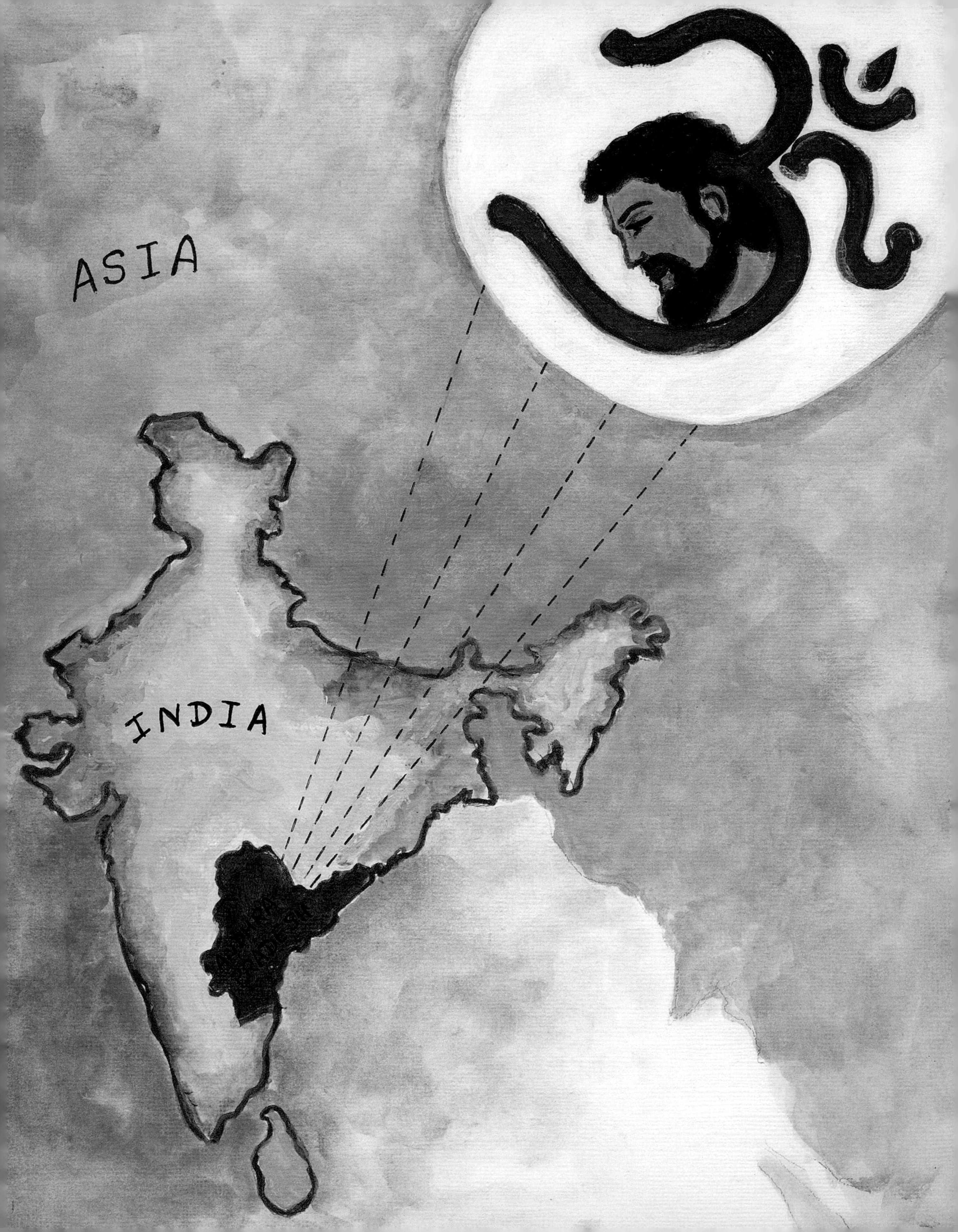
ASIA
INDIA

Who is Vemana?

Vemana is a remarkable medieval poet and a philosopher from around the 17th century. He was born and lived in Andhra Pradesh, India. Andhra or Telugu is the language spoken there and has been called the Italian of the East by some Europeans. Vemana believed in human equality and dreamed of universal brotherhood. The French philosopher Abe Deboy called him the "Andhra Plato".

Almost all Telugu people are familiar with Vemana's extraordinary poetry and grasp the simple and deep moral values in his poems. His expression of ethical philosophy and his fresh analogies are bold and unique. He wrote around 2100 poems in a very spontaneous, humorous, direct and precise way to shed the light of truth.

In this children's storybook, I am attempting to capture and demonstrate a sample of universal values stated beautifully in Vemana's poetry. The ideas in his poetry show his open-mindedness and give us the impression that he might have been at least 300 years ahead of his time. His style is very original and the language he used is remarkably attractive and understandable by everyone. That is why he is referred to as the "Poet of the People".

White Milk

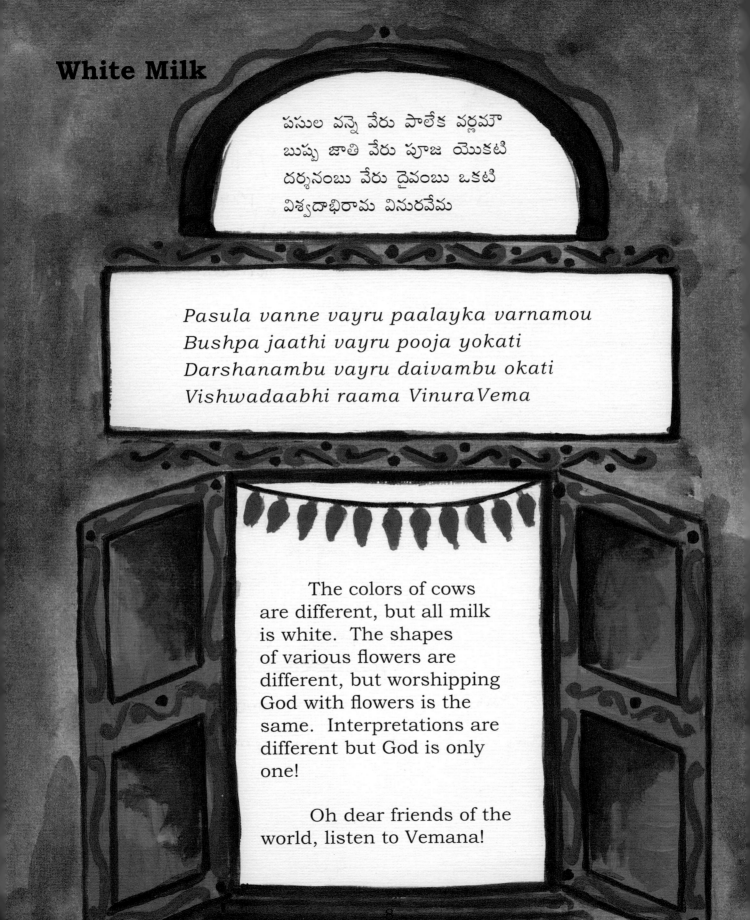

పసుల వన్నె వేరు పాలేక వర్ణమా
బుష్ప జాతి వేరు పూజ యొకటి
దర్శనంబు వేరు దైవంబు ఒకటి
విశ్వదాభిరామ వినురవేమ

Pasula vanne vayru paalayka varnamou
Bushpa jaathi vayru pooja yokati
Darshanambu vayru daivambu okati
Vishwadaabhi raama VinuraVema

The colors of cows are different, but all milk is white. The shapes of various flowers are different, but worshipping God with flowers is the same. Interpretations are different but God is only one!

Oh dear friends of the world, listen to Vemana!

Little Lauren is very excited. She is going with her parents to visit her grandpa at his farm. Once they reach the farm, her grandpa shows her all the cows, horses, pigs and other animals. Lauren sees black cows, brown cows and white cows. She has never seen these different colored cows before.

Grandpa Johnny calls, "Lauren, do you want to come along and watch me milk the cows?" Lauren claps her hands and says, "Oh yes, Grandpa! Let's go!" She watches her grandpa very attentively as he milks the cows, the white cows, the brown cows and the black cows. Lauren is surprised, "Grandpa, why is the milk white even though some cows are black and some are brown?"

Grandpa Johnny tells her, "Sweetie pie, no matter what color the cows are, they all give white milk. Do you know what else?"

"People also have different skin color, but we are all human
beings. Don't ever forget that. No matter what the color, shape and
size each one is, treat everybody with respect and equally nice!"

11

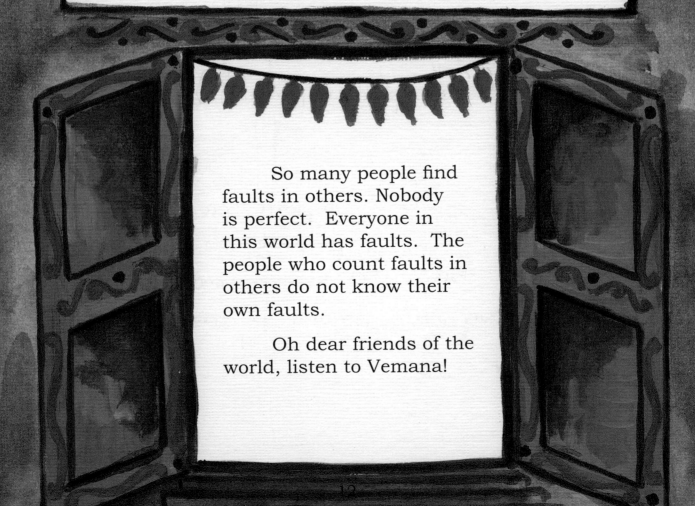

తప్పులెన్నువారు తండోపతండంబు
లుర్వి జనులకెల్ల నుండు దప్పు
తప్పు లెన్నువారు తమ తప్పు లెరుగరు
విశ్వదాభిరామ వినురవేమ

Thappulennuvaaru thandopa thandambu
Lurvijanulakella nundu thappu
Thappulennuvaaru thama thappulerugaru
Vishwadaabhi raama VinuraVema

So many people find faults in others. Nobody is perfect. Everyone in this world has faults. The people who count faults in others do not know their own faults.

Oh dear friends of the world, listen to Vemana!

Sammy got out after her mother stopped the car and walked towards her school. Suddenly, she slipped and fell in a puddle. Luckily she did not get hurt, but her pants were totally wet. Sammy felt so bad she wanted to cry.

At the same time, her friend Amy was dropped off by her mother. When Sammy was about to say hi to her, Amy looked at Sammy and started laughing. She started making fun of Sammy and her wet pants. Now Sammy really felt like crying.

As they were going through the main door, they heard Shawn call out, "Amy, is it a new style to wear a half torn shirt?" Amy said, "What?" Shawn laughed and said, "Look at your back!" Amy found out that her shirt had a big tear in the back, and she didn't even know about it! Here she was making fun of Sammy and her wet pants. She realized that nobody is perfect, and we all have faults of our own. Remember that before finding faults in others or making fun of them.

Stop Arguing

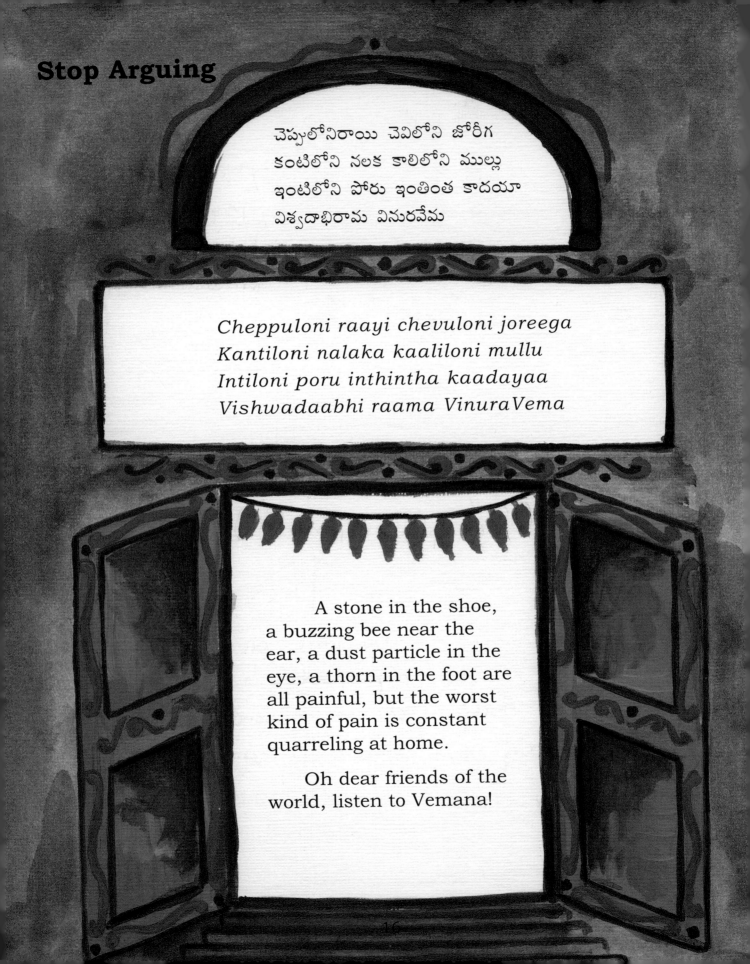

చెప్పులోనిరాయి చెవిలోని జోరీగ
కంటిలోని నలక కాలిలోని ముల్లు
ఇంటిలోని పోరు ఇంతింత కాదయా
విశ్వదాభిరామ వినురవేమ

Cheppuloni raayi chevuloni joreega
Kantiloni nalaka kaaliloni mullu
Intiloni poru inthintha kaadayaa
Vishwadaabhi raama VinuraVema

A stone in the shoe, a buzzing bee near the ear, a dust particle in the eye, a thorn in the foot are all painful, but the worst kind of pain is constant quarreling at home.

Oh dear friends of the world, listen to Vemana!

"Mommy! Mommy! My foot is hurting!" Billy came running inside and showed his foot to his mother in the kitchen. "Where, where is it hurting Billy? Did you twist your foot?" Billy said, "No, Mommy! I think there is something inside my shoe! Get it out, get it out!" "Ok, ok, baby, just wait!" Sally took his shoe off and found a small but sharp rock in his little shoe. She said, "I bet it was hurting, wasn't it?"

As they walked out, they saw their neighbor's daughter Jean, running in her backyard, and saying "Get away from me." They looked to see who Jean was talking to. Nobody was there! Sally said, "Jean, are you all right?" Jean replied, "This bee is following me and making a buzzing noise in my ear!" Sally looked closer. Then she saw that the bee that was following Jean was almost in her ear. Sally chased the bee away with the book she had in her hand.

17

"Sally, Sally, come quick!" Her husband, Dave, who was doing some woodwork in the basement called desperately. "What? What?" She ran down. "Something is in my eye. Can you see, can you get it out please?" Sally looked into his red, watery eye. "I cannot see anything! Maybe you should rinse your eye with water, so whatever is in there will come out."

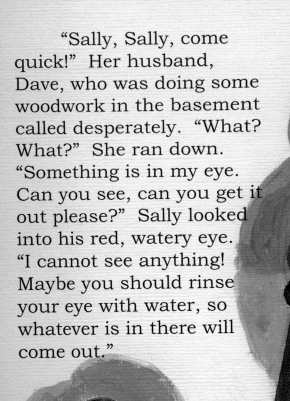

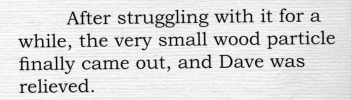

After struggling with it for a while, the very small wood particle finally came out, and Dave was relieved.

Just then, she heard another cry in the backyard. "Ouch!" Her mother yelled in the backyard. Sally stepped outside. "Sally, Can you get this thorn out please, it is really hurting. I had enough gardening for today!" Sally carefully took out the thorn in her mother's foot. Her mother said, "Oh! Much better! That little thorn was hurting so much!"

While they were going in, the doorbell rang. Dave came up and opened the door for his friend Larry to come in. Larry's face was all red! He said, "Dave, let's go and play some tennis. I have to get away!" Dave said, "What's wrong, Larry?" Larry said, "Man, I cannot take it anymore!" Dave asked, "Take what?" Larry said, "Sue and I are never going to stop arguing!" He actually burst into tears.

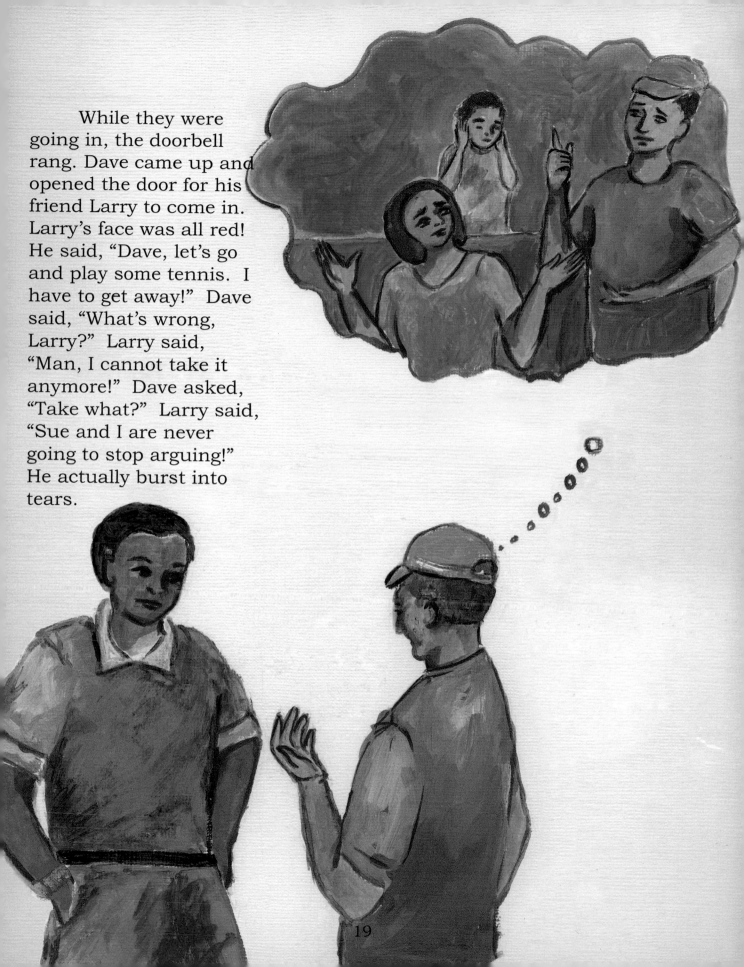

After Dave and Larry left to play tennis, Billy asked, "Mommy, why is Uncle Larry crying?" Sally answered, "Because arguments at home are hurting him and his wife Sue. You see, Honey, constant quarreling is more painful than a stone in the shoe, a buzzing bee near the ear, a dust particle in the eye, and even a thorn in the foot. We all need to learn to be calm and communicate in a loving way, rather than argue all the time! Always remember that, Ok?" Billy said, "Ok, Mommy!"

Sharing is Important

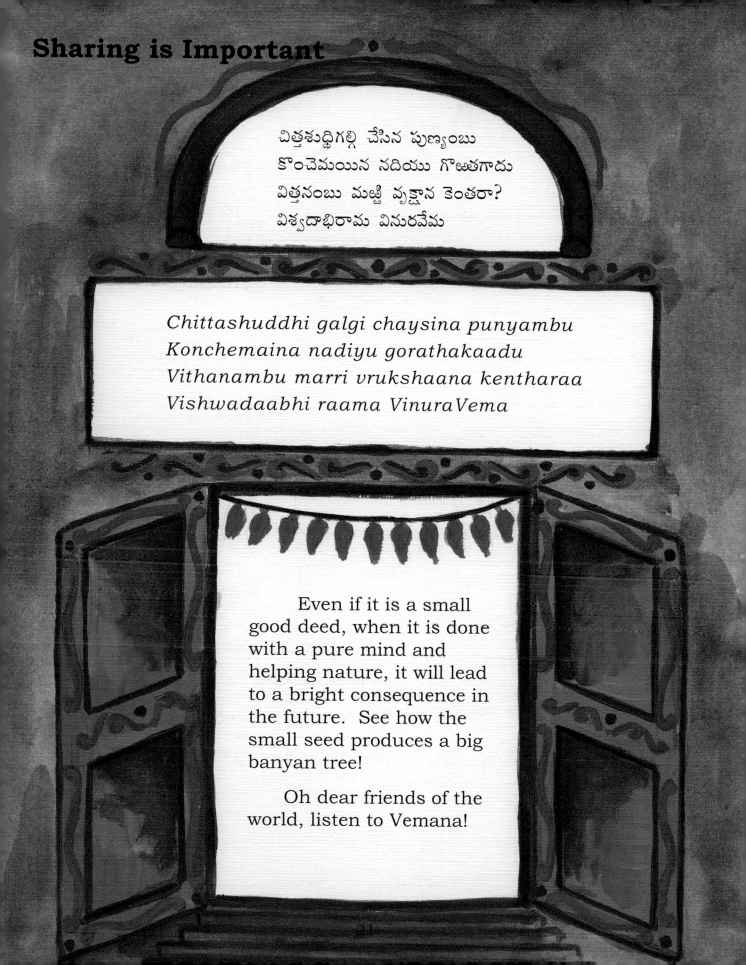

చిత్తశుద్ధిగల్గి చేసిన పుణ్యంబు
కొంచెమయిన నదియు గోఉతగాదు
విత్తనంబు మట్టి వృక్షాన కెంతరా?
విశ్వదాభిరామ వినురవేమ

Chittashuddhi galgi chaysina punyambu
Konchemaina nadiyu gorathakaadu
Vithanambu marri vrukshaana kentharaa
Vishwadaabhi raama VinuraVema

Even if it is a small good deed, when it is done with a pure mind and helping nature, it will lead to a bright consequence in the future. See how the small seed produces a big banyan tree!

Oh dear friends of the world, listen to Vemana!

21

Kelly has a swing set in her backyard. She enjoys playing in the backyard along with her brother, Tom. Susan is Kelly's next-door neighbor. She has no swing set in her backyard. One day Kelly asked her mother, "Mommy, can Susan play with me in our backyard? I feel sorry for her because she has no swing set in her backyard." Margaret said, "Sure sweetheart! Make sure that it is OK with Susan's mother." With Susan's mother's permission, Kelly and Susan had fun swinging.

That night after dinner, Margaret showed a seed to Kelly and said, "Kelly, I am very proud of you for your kind gesture to share your swing set with Susan. Do you see that big tree in our backyard? It grew from a small seed like this."

"Today, your kind gesture towards Susan is like a small seed that you planted, and out of it can grow a very strong friendship that lasts your entire life! When you grow up, you both may be doing a lot more fun and useful things together."

Be Humble

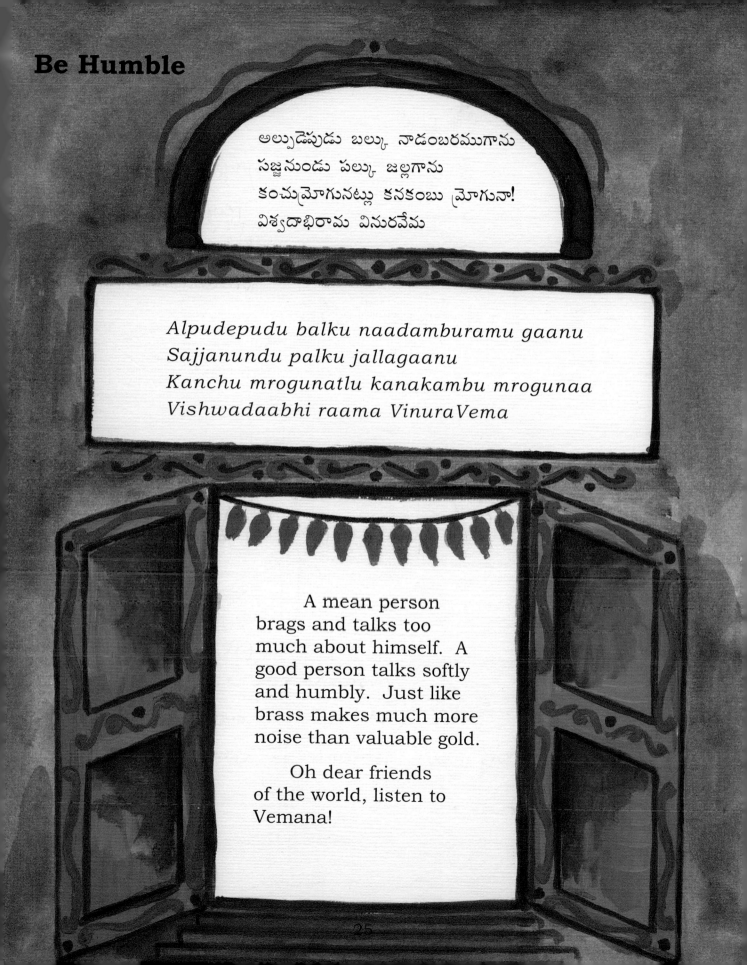

అల్పుడెపుడు బల్కు నాడంబరముగాను
సజ్జనుండు పల్కు జల్లగాను
కంచుమోగునట్లు కనకంబు మ్రోగునా!
విశ్వదాభిరామ వినురవేమ

Alpudepudu balku naadamburamu gaanu
Sajjanundu palku jallagaanu
Kanchu mrogunatlu kanakambu mrogunaa
Vishwadaabhi raama VinuraVema

A mean person brags and talks too much about himself. A good person talks softly and humbly. Just like brass makes much more noise than valuable gold.

Oh dear friends of the world, listen to Vemana!

"Naanana naana! I got a B+! You got only a C-! Haha haha! I am better than you!" Kris was waving his paper by Ram's face. Ram was about to cry. He ran to his mother.

Their mother comforted Ram and said to Kris, "It is not nice to make fun of your brother or anybody. He may get a better grade than you next time. Come on boys, let's have dinner." Anita, her husband Steve and their twin sons sat down for dinner. Just as they finished eating and put things away, Ashley, from next door, came and rang the door bell. "Hi! Do you guys want to play a board game?" Ashley asked Kris and Ram. "Yeah, Yeah!" Ram went and got their new board game, and they started playing.

Steve came to Ashley and said, "Congratulations Ashley! Your dad told me that you won the State Spelling Bee."

Ashley said "Thank you!" Kris
said, "Is that the spelling bee that I
lost in the first round?" Steve said,
"Yes Kris. Ashley was the spelling bee champion for your school,
our region, our city, and our whole
state. Isn't that great?"

That night when the twin boys were going to bed, Anita said, "Did you see, Kris? Ashley did not even brag about her spelling bee championship. You should never brag about yourself. Earlier this evening, you were boasting about your grade in math. Other people should speak about your great deeds, not you. You know who talks about himself a lot? A shallow person who does not really have great qualities talks about himself a lot. A person who is really great talks well about others, not himself. Do you understand baby?" Kris said, "Yes Mommy!" Ram said, "Mommy, wasn't it nice that Ashley didn't even brag about her winning, and she didn't make fun of us losing in the first round?" Anita said, "You are right! She is nice! Good night guys and sweet dreams!"

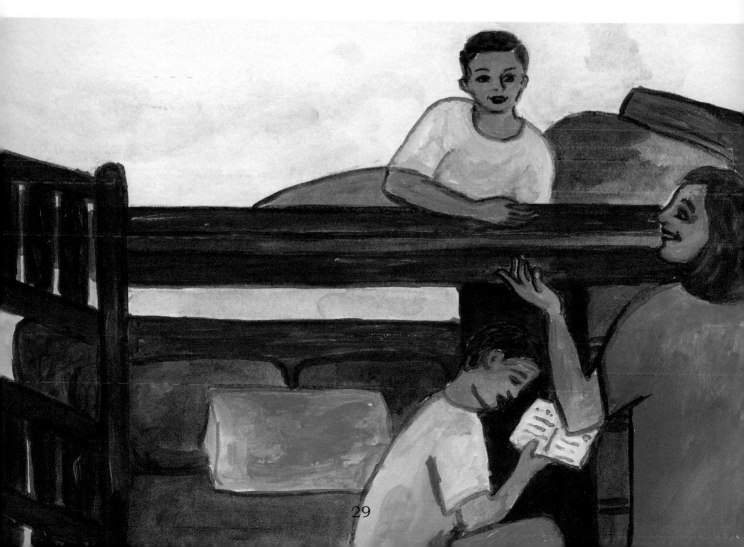

Universal values are the same

Remember and follow these important messages throughout your life, and you will shine in this world!

1. **Equality:** Even though the outside colors are different, the inner truth is the same. You get what you give. So give respect, and you will get respect.

2. **Kindness:** Be kind to others. Nobody is perfect. Help them but don't criticize (or point fingers). If you are kind, the whole world will be kind to you. So treat everyone the way you want to be treated!

3. **Harmony:** Arguing and fighting is more painful than any other kind of pain! It does not solve anything. Find ways to resolve differences without fighting. Happiness comes from harmony.

4. **Sharing:** Whatever you are blessed with, share with others. A small gesture today is like a seed which will grow and become a big tree later. You can enjoy the fruits from that tree in your future!

5. **Be humble:** Everybody is good at something! Being humble is part of being great. We should not brag about ourselves. Look for and admire small and big qualities in others.

Pronunciations and Definitions

The Author

Sita Mutyala was born and raised in India and has been living in the United States since 1967. She has a bachelors degree in Computer Science, a CPA and an Executive MBA. She happily retired after 33 years as an IT professional. Her interests include painting, writing, traveling, vocal music, playing the veena, acting, sewing, and enjoying family and friends. Sita has a daughter and a son and is the proud grandmother of one grandson and two granddaughters. She lives with her husband in Sugar Land, Texas and her current passion is service for elders.

By this children's book, she hopes to spread Eastern spiritual values that she brought from her roots in Andhra Pradesh, India, and especially the moral gems by Vemana, to her Western homeland. She feels that even if one child benefits from the messages in this book, all of her efforts in publishing it are worth while! You can contact Mrs. Sita Mutyala at WeShinePress@yahoo.com.

The Illustrator

Sireesha Amaram is originally from India but has lived in the United States since 1977. She currently resides in Houston, Texas. While she has degrees in Biology from both India and the U.S., she has had a lifelong passion for the arts and has spent numerous years as an artist.

She works in oil, pastel, watercolor, and acrylics. Her paintings focus primarily on the people and architecture of India but her interest in all cultures and people of the world is reflected in her work. When she is not painting, she enjoys gardening, reading, and spending time with family and friends. To contact Sireesha, please e-mail her at s_amaram@yahoo.com.

WeShine Press Co